METUSELA ALBERT

WHO IS SITTING ON THE THRONE, IN HEAVEN? JESUS, THE ONLY GOD.

To order additional copies of this book, contact:
Xlibris
844-714-8691
www.Xlibris.com
Orders@Xlibris.com

ISBN: Softcover   979-8-3694-3138-2
         EBook   979-8-3694-3139-9

Print information available on the last page

Rev. date: 10/04/2024

Contents

– REVELATION 4:1-11; REVELATION 21:5-7.

LET'S READ REVELATION 4:1-11.

1. After this I looked, and, behold, a door was opened in heaven: and the first voice which I heard was as it were of a trumpet talking with me; which said, Come up hither, and I will shew thee things which must be hereafter.

[2] And immediately I was in the spirit: and, behold, <u>behold, a throne was set in heaven</u>, and <u>one sat on the throne</u>.

[3] And <u>he that sat was to look upon like a jasper and a sardine stone</u>: and there was a rainbow round about the throne, in sight like unto an emerald.

[4] And round about the throne were four and twenty seats: and upon the seats I saw four and twenty elders sitting, clothed in white raiment; and they had on their heads crowns of gold.

[5] And out of the throne proceeded lightnings and thunderings and voices: and there were seven lamps of fire burning before the throne, which are the seven Spirits of God.

⁶ And before the throne there was a sea of glass like unto crystal: and in the midst of the throne, and round about the throne, were four beasts full of eyes before and behind.

⁷ And the <u>first beast</u> was like <u>a lion</u>, and the <u>second beast</u> like a <u>calf</u>, and <u>the third beast</u> had <u>a face as a man</u>, and <u>the fourth beast</u> was like <u>a flying eagle</u>.

⁸ And the four beasts had each of them six wings about him; and they were full of eyes within: and they rest not day and night, <u>saying, Holy, holy, holy, Lord God Almighty, which was, and is, and is to come.</u>

⁹ And when those beasts give glory and honour and thanks <u>to him that sat on the throne, who liveth for ever and ever,</u>

¹⁰ The four and twenty elders fall down <u>before him that sat on the throne, and worship him that liveth for ever and ever, and cast their crowns before the throne, saying,</u>

¹¹ <u>Thou art worthy, O Lord, to receive glory and honour and power: for thou hast created all things, and for thy pleasure they are and were created.</u>

....
....
....
....

Let's read our <u>second Scripture Reading</u> – Revelation 21:5-7.

....
....
....
....

NOTE: The One that is sitting on the THRONE, in heaven, is called – <u>Alpha and Omega</u>, <u>the First and the Last.</u>

HE IS JESUS, THE ELOHIM, WHO CREATED HEAVEN AND EARTH IN SIX DAYS AND RESTED ON THE SEVENTH DAY.

NOTE: The One on the Throne is <u>NOT</u> a Trinity GOD, NEITHER a Duality GOD.

....
....
....
....

FURTHERMORE, THE HOLY SPIRIT IS <u>NOT</u> A THIRD PERSON.

THEREFORE, THE BOTTOM-LINE IS – SINCE JESUS WAS THE GOD OF ABRAHAM, THAT MEANS, THE GOD OF ABRAHAM, ISAAC, AND JACOB, DID NOT HAVE A BEGOTTEN SON CALLED - JESUS, IN HEAVEN.

OF COURSE, GOD GAVE BIRTH TO NO BEGOTTEN SON, CALLED – JESUS, IN HEAVEN.

DEAR READER,

THERE WAS NO SON OF GOD CALLED – "JESUS," THAT EVER EXISTED IN HEAVEN, BEFORE THE ANGELS WERE CREATED.

....
....
....
....

THAT IS A CENTRAL TRUTH THAT MOST MAINLINE DENOMINATIONS WITH MILLIONS OF MEMBERS, STILL HAVE NOT UNDERSTOOD YET. EVEN THE PASTORS AND ELDERS, OF THOSE CHURCHES, ARE STILL IN THE LOOP HOLE. THEY DON'T KNOW THAT THEY ARE BELIEVING IN A LIE ADVOCATED BY THEIR OWN CHURCHES.

IF THEY DID NOT UDERSTAND THAT CENTRAL TRUTH YET, THEN YOU CAN IMAGINE THE GREAT APOSTASY WITHIN THE CHURCHES AND THE MEMBERS.

....
....
....
....

THE BELIEF THAT SAYS, "GOD HAD A BEGOTTEN SON CALLED, JESUS, IN HEAVEN, BEFORE THE ANGELS EXISTED," IS ANTI-CHRIST.

HOW?

IN FACT, THAT BELIEF IS <u>ANTI-CHRIST</u> BECAUSE IT <u>DEMOTED</u> JESUS, WHO WAS A SELF-EXISTENT GOD, WHO WAS <u>THE "ELOHIM"</u> WHO CREATED HEAVEN AND EARTH; TO A CREATURE, WITH A BEGINNING. THAT BELIEF <u>DENIED</u> JESUS CHRIST, AS THE ALPHA AND OMEGA, THE FIRST AND THE LAST.

Dear folks, DO Not Buy the LIE of the TRINITY GOD, theory. DO Not Buy the LIE of the Mainline Denominations. Stop demoting your self-existent GOD, to a creature with a beginning.

....

....

....

....

INTRODUCTION

When you have a good understanding that JESUS CHRIST was the "<u>ELOHIM</u>" who created heaven and earth in six days and rested on the seventh day, who later came in human flesh through Mary at Bethlehem; easily you would have known that <u>HE alone has to be the One sitting on the THRONE, in heaven.</u> Common sense and Logic Thinking would have helped you make that Realistic Conclusion; even without reading Revelation Chapter 4.

Reading Revelation Chapter 4:1-11, only affirms the truth about JESUS as the only GOD who exists from eternity, the Alpha and Omega, who is sitting on the Throne, in heaven. Of course, Revelation Chapter 4:1-11, cannot contradict what GOD said to the Prophet, in Isaiah 43:10-11. It is that simple. You cannot read Scripture without reasoning in a logical manner.

....
....
....
....

CHAPTER 1

JESUS WAS <u>THE ELOHIM</u>, WHO CREATED HEAVEN AND EARTH.

Genesis 1:1 says, In the beginning <u>God</u> created the heaven and the earth. (KJV).

NOTE: The Bible begins by introducing "GOD", as <u>the CREATOR</u> of heaven and earth. In the Hebrew Bible, the word used for "<u>GOD</u>" is "<u>ELOHIM</u>". Therefore, "<u>ELOHIM</u>" was the CREATOR. The Spanish word is – "<u>DIOS."</u>

WORSHIP IS DUE TO <u>ELOHIM</u>, THE CREATOR. THAT IS WHY THE FIRST COMMANDMENT IN THE TEN COMMANDMENTS, TELLS US TO WORSHIP HIM ALONE – (Exodus 20:1-3).

....
....
....
....

In John 5:39, JESUS said, <u>Search the Scriptures</u>; for them ye think ye have eternal life, <u>but they are they which testify of Me.</u>

In John 5:46, JESUS said, Had you believed Moses, you would have believed <u>Me;</u> for Moses wrote about <u>Me.</u>

....
....
....
....

In John 5:39 and 46, JESUS told the disciples that HE was the <u>ELOHIM</u> whom Moses wrote in the first five Books of the Old Testament – Genesis, Exodus, Leviticus, Numbers, and Deuteronomy – (THE TORAH).

In John 5:58, JESUS said, <u>Before Abraham was I am.</u>

<u>NOTE: JESUS DECLARED THAT HE EXISTED BEFORE ABRAHAM. In other words, HE was the GOD of Abraham.</u>

The Jews often claimed that the GOD of Abraham was their GOD; yet failed to realize that JESUS who was in human flesh through Mary was the GOD of Abraham. Sadly, the words of JESUS fell into deaf ears. The Jews failed to evaluate the Prophecies written in the Book of Isaiah in reference to the Messiah's coming through a virgin woman – (Isaiah 9:6; 7:14).

IN WHAT WAY, WE AS PROFESSED CHRISTIANS ARE REPEATING THE MISTAKE OF THE JEWISH PEOPLE?

While we claim to believe in JESUS, yet we failed to recognize Him as the GOD of Abraham who came in human flesh through Mary at Bethlehem. Thus, we continue to believe in a TRINITY GOD theory. In fact, we are worse than the JEWS who killed JESUS because we failed to understand Scripture. The Trinity GOD theory is Anti-Christ. It demoted JESUS, the ALPHA AND OMEGA, to a Creature with a beginning.

Most Professed Christians don't realize it; and that is the reason this Book is written to provoke our minds to reason things in a stronger way. We should challenge our Traditional doctrines that speak about a TRINITY GOD with a Begotten Son.

....

....

....

....

**"ELOHIM"
CREATED HEAVEN AND EARTH.**

**JESUS WAS THE "ELOHIM" WHO
CREATED HEAVEN AND EARTH.**

**THEREFORE, JESUS WHO WAS
"ELOHIM,"
DID NOT HAVE A BEGOTTEN SON
CALLED - JESUS.**

....
....
....
....

CHAPTER 2

JESUS WAS THE <u>GOD</u> OF NOAH.

Read Genesis Chapter 6 and learn of the conversation between GOD and Noah. The GOD who spoke to Noah for him to build the Ark, was <u>not</u> a Trinity GOD. Try and take note of the Singular Pronouns used in reference to GOD.

LET'S READ GENESIS CHAPTER 6:1-22.

1. And it came to pass, when men began to multiply on the face of the earth, and daughters were born unto them,

² That the sons of God saw the daughters of men that they were fair; and they took them wives of all which they chose.

³ And <u>the Lord said</u>, <u>My</u> spirit shall not always strive with man, for that he also is flesh: yet his days shall be an hundred and twenty years.

⁴ There were giants in the earth in those days; and also after that, when the sons of <u>God</u> came in unto the daughters of men, and they bare children to them, the same became mighty men which were of old, men of renown.

⁵ And <u>God</u> saw that the wickedness of man was great in the earth, and that every imagination of the thoughts of his heart was only evil continually.

⁶ And it repented <u>the Lord</u> that <u>he</u> had made man on the earth, and it grieved <u>him</u> at <u>his</u> heart.

⁷ And <u>the Lord said, I will destroy man whom I have created</u> from the face of the earth; both man, and beast, and the creeping thing, and the fowls of the air; <u>for it repenteth me that I have made them</u>.

⁸ But Noah found grace in the eyes of <u>the Lord.</u>

⁹ These are the generations of Noah: Noah was a just man and perfect in his generations, and Noah walked with <u>God.</u>

¹⁰ And Noah begat three sons, Shem, Ham, and Japheth.

¹¹ The earth also was corrupt before <u>God</u>, and the earth was filled with violence.

¹² And <u>God</u> looked upon the earth, and, behold, it was corrupt; for all flesh had corrupted his way upon the earth.

¹³ And <u>God</u> said unto Noah, The end of all flesh is come before <u>me</u>; for the earth is filled with violence through them; and, behold<u>, I will</u> destroy them with the earth.

¹⁴ Make thee an ark of gopher wood; rooms shalt thou make in the ark, and shalt pitch it within and without with pitch.

¹⁵ And this is the fashion which thou shalt make it of: The length of the ark shall be three hundred cubits, the breadth of it fifty cubits, and the height of it thirty cubits.

¹⁶ A window shalt thou make to the ark, and in a cubit shalt thou finish it above; and the door of the ark shalt thou set in the side thereof; with lower, second, and third stories shalt thou make it.

¹⁷ And, behold, I, even I, do bring a flood of waters upon the earth, to destroy all flesh, wherein is the breath of life, from under heaven; and every thing that is in the earth shall die.

¹⁸ But with thee will I establish my covenant; and thou shalt come into the ark, thou, and thy sons, and thy wife, and thy sons' wives with thee.

¹⁹ And of every living thing of all flesh, two of every sort shalt thou bring into the ark, to keep them alive with thee; they shall be male and female.

²⁰ Of fowls after their kind, and of cattle after their kind, of every creeping thing of the earth after his kind, two of every sort shall come unto thee, to keep them alive.

²¹ And take thou unto thee of all food that is eaten, and thou shalt gather it to thee; and it shall be for food for thee, and for them.

²² Thus did Noah; according to all that God commanded him, so did he.

....
....
....
....

Who is Sitting on the Throne, in Heaven? Jesus, the Only God.

7

GENESIS 6:3, 6 & 7. THE SINGULAR PRONOUNS FOR GOD

- ³ And <u>the Lord said</u>, <u>My</u> spirit shall not always strive with man, for that he also is flesh: yet his days shall be an hundred and twenty years.

- ⁶ And it repented <u>the Lord</u> that <u>he</u> had made man on the earth, and it grieved <u>him</u> at <u>his</u> heart.

- ⁷ And <u>the Lord said</u>, <u>I will</u> <u>destroy man whom I have created</u> from the face of the earth; both man, and beast, and the creeping thing, and the fowls of the air; <u>for it repenteth me that I have made them.</u>

Did you notice the <u>Singular Pronouns</u> used in Genesis 6:3, 6-7? –

Verse 3. MY.

Verse 6. HE, HIS, HIM.

Verse 7. ME, I (3 times).

THEREFORE, THE GOD OF NOAH WAS <u>NOT</u> A TRINITY GOD.

....
....
....
....

CHAPTER 3

JESUS WAS THE GOD OF ABRAHAM.

Read Genesis 12:1-3; Exodus 3:13-14; John 5:39, 46; 8:56-58.

....
....
....
....

THE GOD OF ABRAHAM WAS<u>NOT</u> A TRINITY GOD

- Genesis 12:1-3.(King James Version).

- 1. Now **the LORD** had said unto Abram, "Get thee out of thy country, and from thy kindred and from thy father's house, unto a land that **I** will show thee.

- ² And **I** will make of thee a great nation, and **I** will bless thee and make thy name great; and thou shalt be a blessing.

- ³ And **I** will bless them that bless thee, and curse him that curseth thee; and in thee shall all families of the earth be blessed."

DID YOU NOTICE THAT THE PRONOUN "I" WAS MENTIONED FOUR (4) TIMES? . . . . NOT "WE"

Compiled by: Metusela F. Albert

....
....
....
....

Exodus 3:13-14.

JESUS was the <u>I AM THAT I AM</u> who spoke to Moses at the Burning Bush.

In John 5:39, JESUS said – Search the Scriptures, for in them ye think ye have eternal life; but they are they which testify of Me.

NOTE: At time when JESUS made the statement, the Scripture was <u>the Old Testament</u>. There was no New Testament written yet. Therefore, the GOD mentioned in the Old Testament was JESUS.

JESUS also said in John 5:46, Had ye believed Moses, ye would have believed <u>me</u>; for Moses <u>wrote about me</u>.

NOTE: Moses wrote <u>the first five Books</u> of the Old Testament. That is – Genesis, Exodus, Leviticus, Numbers, and Deuteronomy.

When you read about <u>GOD</u> (JEHOVAH / YAHWEH) as mentioned in those five Books that Moses wrote, that would be JESUS before his incarnation into human flesh at Bethlehem through Mary. Therefore, JESUS was the only GOD who spoke to the Prophets in the Old Testament era.

The 66 Books of the Old Testament testify of <u>One GOD</u>, <u>the Creator</u> of heaven and earth; the GOD of Abraham, Isaac, and Jacob. HE was none other than JESUS CHRIST who later came in human flesh through Mary at Bethlehem, by the INCARNATION process. There was no GOD before and after Him – Isaiah 43:10-11, 15.

//
//
//
//

THE GOD OF ABRAHAM DID NOT HAVE A SON IN HEAVEN CALLED - JESUS.

NOTE: JESUS WAS THE GOD OF ABRAHAM WHO HUMBLY TOOK HUMAN FLESH THROUGH MARY AT BETHLEHEM.

THIS WAS THE INCARNATION PROCESS.

Read - Genesis 1:1-31; 2:1-3; Exodus 3:13-14;6:1-3; Isaiah 43:10-11; 44:6, 24; 49:16; John 5:39, 46; 8:56-58; Revelation 21:6-7.

CHAPTER 4

JESUS WAS THE <u>I AM THAT I AM</u> WHO SPOKE TO MOSES AT THE BURNING BUSH.

Read Exodus 3:13-14; John 5:39, 46-47; 8:56-58.

It was "ELOHIM" who took Human Flesh through Mary at Bethlehem by <u>the INCARNATION process</u>, AND BECAME THE SON OF GOD, to die at calvary as our Sin Bearer / Savior. HIS NAME IS – "JESUS".

READ – Genesis 1:1-31; 2:1-3; Exodus 3:13-14; 6:1-3; Isaiah 43:10-11; 44:6, 24; 49:16; John 5:39, 46; 8:56-58; Revelation 21:6-7.

Compiled by: Metusela F. Albert.

....
....
....
....

CHAPTER 5

JESUS WAS THE <u>ELOHIM</u> WHO WROTE THE TEN COMMANDMENTS.

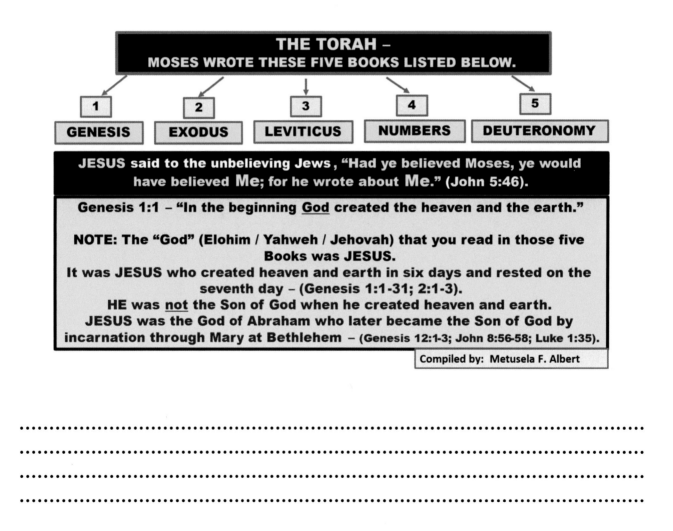

THE TORAH –
MOSES WROTE THESE FIVE BOOKS LISTED BELOW.

1	2	3	4	5
GENESIS	**EXODUS**	**LEVITICUS**	**NUMBERS**	**DEUTERONOMY**

JESUS said to the unbelieving Jews, "Had ye believed Moses, ye would have believed **Me**; for he wrote about **Me**." (John 5:46).

Genesis 1:1 – "In the beginning <u>God</u> created the heaven and the earth."

NOTE: The "God" (Elohim / Yahweh / Jehovah) that you read in those five Books was JESUS.
It was JESUS who created heaven and earth in six days and rested on the seventh day – (Genesis 1:1-31; 2:1-3).
HE was <u>not</u> the Son of God when he created heaven and earth.
JESUS was the God of Abraham who later became the Son of God by incarnation through Mary at Bethlehem – (Genesis 12:1-3; John 8:56-58; Luke 1:35).

Compiled by: Metusela F. Albert

THE <u>THREE BOOKS</u> SHOWING BELOW EXPLAINS IN DETAIL ABOUT JESUS CHRIST IN THE OLD TESTAMENT ERA. THERE WAS NO TRINITY GOD IN HEAVEN.

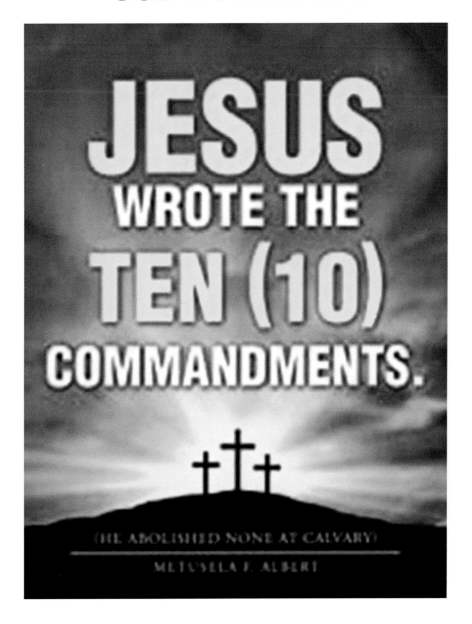

....
....
....
....

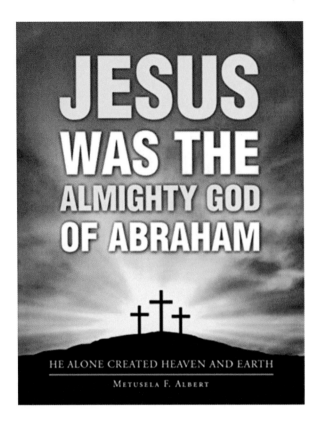

....
....
....
....

JESUS, IS THE <u>ONLY GOD,</u> THAT IS SITTING ON THE THRONE, IN HEAVEN.

....

....

....

....

CHAPTER 6

JESUS WAS THE <u>ELOHIM</u> WHO SPOKE TO PROPHET ISAIAH.

Read Isaiah 43:10-11; 15; 49:16; 53:1-10; 9:6; 7:14; Matthew 1:21-23.

- **SCRIPTURE READING – ISAIAH 43:10 - 11.**

-

- **v10. Ye are <u>my</u> witnesses, <u>saith the LORD</u>, and <u>my</u> servant whom <u>I</u> have choses: that ye may know and believe <u>me</u>, and understand <u>that I am he</u>: <u>before me there was no God formed, neither shall there be after me</u>**

- **v11. I, even I, am the LORD; <u>and beside me there is no Savior.</u>**

-

- **v15<u>. I am the LORD, your Holy One, the creator of Israel, your King.</u>**

Compiled by: Metusela F. Albert.

NOTE: When the Bible Student understands fully the meaning of this Scripture mentioned above, he or she will not believe again in the False teaching called - TRINITY GOD.

Furthermore, the Bible Student will not believe in the DUALITY GOD, in John 1:1-3 and John 3:16, because those Scriptures contradicted Genesis 1:1 and Isaiah 43:10-11, 15.

The same Bible Student will <u>not</u> believe in Colossians 1:15-18 as written by Paul, because it contradicted Genesis 1:1 and Isaiah 43:10-11, 15.

....

....

....

....

I want to remind the reader of this Book. If you continue to believe that GOD the Father, had a Begotten Son, in heaven, before the angels were created, thus, you have incorrectly made JESUS, to be a creature with a beginning; yet He was the only Self-Existent GOD, who created heaven and earth.

....

....

....

....

CHAPTER 7

JESUS WAS THE <u>ELOHIM</u> WHO INCARNATED INTO HUMAN FLESH, AND DIED AT CALVARY.

Isaiah 9:6; 7:14; Matthew 1:21-23.

EMMANUEL, THE PRINCE OF PEACE, TOOK HUMAN FLESH AND DWELT AMONG THE JEWS AND THE GENTILES.

It was "ELOHIM" who took Human Flesh through Mary at Bethlehem by the <u>INCARNATION</u> process,
AND
BECAME THE SON OF GOD,
to die at calvary as our Sin Bearer / Savior.
HIS NAME IS – "JESUS".

READ – Genesis 1:1-31; 2:1-3; Exodus 3:13-14; 6:1-3; Isaiah 43:10-11; 44:6, 24; 49:16; John 5:39, 46; 8:56-58; Revelation 21:6-7.

Compiled by: Metusela F. Albert.

....

....

....

....

//

//

//

//

CHAPTER 8

WHY ELOHIM INCARNATED INTO HUMAN FLESH, TO DIE AT CALVARY?

Read Genesis 2:16-17; 3:1-10.

When Adam and Eve disobeyed GOD'S command and ate of the fruit from the TREE of the Knowledge of Good and Evil; they openly transgressed GOD'S law. They believed Satan instead of GOD, who created them.

....
....
....
....

SEVEN MAIN REASONS WHY ELOHIM INCARNATED INTO HUMAN FLESH, TO DIE AT CALVARY.

 # 1 – The Sin offering to pay for the penalty of Sin, has to be the life of the Law-Giver. A Lamb Offering is _not_ sufficient.

 # 2 – Since the Law-Giver was an everlasting GOD, HE cannot die. Therefore, HE WAS INCARNATED through Mary, to enable Him to die.

3 – The Law-Giver must take up human flesh to prove that Adam and Eve had the potential to obey GOD.

4 – To prove that all human beings who inherited Adam and Eve's Sinful Nature can faithfully keep GOD'S HOLY LAW when they abide in JESUS. SINLESSNESS IS POSSIBLE. (John 14:15; Matthew 5:48).

5 – To prove that whosoever continues to live in Sin, will **not** be Saved. JESUS came to save us *from* Sin, NOT save us *in* Sin.

6 – To prove that Obedience to GOD'S law, <u>is a condition to enter heaven</u>.

7 – To prove that Salvation is through JESUS CHRIST; not by the law.

NOTE: JESUS IS THE SAVIOR. THE LAW IS <u>NOT</u> THE SAVIOR.

REMEMBER: JESUS IS THE SAVIOR. NO DENOMINATION IS THE SAVIOR.

HERE IS THE TRUTH: NOBODY NEEDS TO BELONG TO A CERTAIN DENOMINATION TO BE SAVED, OR TO BE PART OF GOD'S REMNANT CHURCH.

The sacrifice to pay the penalty of sin has to be the life of the Law-giver. No angel could become the sin offering sacrifice.

Since GOD is self-existent, HE cannot die, thus He must be <u>INCARNATED</u> into human flesh, to allow him to die as mankind's Sin Bearer / Savior.

ELOHIM came in human flesh to show us how to keep His law, because the law can be kept holy. There is no excuse by man that the law cannot be kept holy. Therefore, JESUS became our example in how to keep GOD'S law. Without Him, we can do nothing. But with Christ abiding in us, we can keep GOD'S law holy. (1 John 3:4–9). Amen!

THE MOST AMAZING LOVE STORY ABOUT GOD WHO BECAME HUMAN FLESH THROUGH MARY AT BETHLEHEM, TO SAVE MANKIND FROM SIN, AND TO GIVE MANKIND ETERNAL LIFE.

....
....
....
....

///
///
///
///

CHAPTER 9

ELOHIM DID <u>NOT</u> HAVE A BEGOTTEN SON, CALLED – <u>JESUS</u>, IN HEAVEN.

Most Professed Christians do not understand this doctrine about JESUS. I urge the Reader, to stay tuned and follow me well, as I share this truth with you.

THE ANGELS IN HEAVEN DID <u>NOT</u> KNOW OF A SON OF GOD CALLED JESUS, EXISTED IN HEAVEN. THEY ONLY KNEW GOD.

In heaven, Lucifer <u>wanted to be like GOD</u>. It was <u>not,</u> Lucifer wanted to be like the Son of GOD. . . . There was no Son of GOD, in heaven. Did you get it? I hope you realize the apostasy told by most Churches about GOD and His Begotten Son, that existed in heaven, from eternity.

To believe that GOD THE FATHER had a Begotten SON, in heaven, from eternity, IS TO BELIEVE IN A DUALITY GOD THEORY.

THE UNKNOWN TRUTH ABOUT JESUS, IS:

THE GOD OF ABRAHAM DID NOT HAVE A SON IN HEAVEN CALLED - JESUS.

NOTE: JESUS WAS THE GOD OF ABRAHAM WHO HUMBLY TOOK HUMAN FLESH THROUGH MARY AT BETHLEHEM.

THIS WAS THE INCARNATION PROCESS.

Read - Genesis 1:1-31; 2:1-3; Exodus 3:13-14;6:1-3; Isaiah 43:10-11; 44:6, 24; 49:16; John 5:39, 46; 8:56-58; Revelation 21:6-7.

NOTE: When Professed Christians continue to believe in a TRINITY GOD THEORY, hence this truth about JESUS, becomes foreign to their understanding. The INCARNATION doctrine becomes foreign also. And they lack understanding of the One who is sitting on the Throne, in heaven.

///
///
///
///

CHAPTER 10

ELOHIM IS COMING BACK TO TAKE HIS CHURCH, <u>NOT</u> TAKING A DENOMINATION.

GOD'S CHURCH IS MADE UP OF INDIVIDUAL PEOPLE WHO LOVE GOD AND KEEP HIS COMMANDMENTS. THEY ARE <u>NOT</u> MEMBERS OF ONE PARTICULAR CHURCH OR A DENOMINATION. . . . GOD KNOWS WHO THEY ARE.

....
....
....
....

TAKE NOTE THAT GOD'S CHURCH IS <u>NOT</u> A DENOMINATION THAT CLAIMS TO BE GOD'S CHURCH. THEREFORE, AVOID BEING DECEIVED BY DENOMINATIONS THAT MAKE THE CLAIM THAT THEY ARE THE TRUE CHURCH OF GOD.

LET ME BE MORE SPECIFIC, SO THAT YOU ARE NOT DECEIVED ANYMORE FROM TODAY.

1. THE SEVENTH DAY ADVENTIST (SDA) CHURCH THAT WAS FOUNDED BY MRS. ELLEN G. WHITE IN 1863 A.D., IS <u>NOT</u> GOD'S CHURCH.
2. THE PENTECOSTAL CHURCH, IS <u>NOT</u> GOD'S CHURCH.
3. THE ASSEBLIES OF GOD (AOG) CHURCH, IS <u>NOT</u> GOD'S CHURCH.
4. THE CHURCH OF JESUS CHRIST, IS <u>NOT</u> GOD'S CHURCH.

5. THE LATTER-DAY SAINTS CHURCH, IS NOT GOD'S CHURCH.
6. THE MORMON CHURCH, IS NOT GOD'S CHURCH.
7. THE 7TH DAY ADVENT BIBLE MINISTRY CHURCH, IS NOT GOD'S CHURCH.
8. THE 7TH DAY BAPTIST CHURCH, IS NOT GOD'S CHURCH.
9. THE WORLWIDE CHURCH OF GOD, IS NOT GOD'S CHURCH.
10. THE METHODIST CHURCH, IS NOT GOD'S CHURCH.
11. THE NEW METHODIST CHURCH, IS NOT GOD'S CHURCH.
12. THE FAMILY WORSHIP CENTER BY JIMMY SWAGGART, IS NOT GOD'S CHURCH.
13. THE CHURCH OF JOEL OSTEIN, IS NOT GOD'S CHURCH.
14. THE CHURCH OF T.D. JAKES, IS NOT GOD'S CHURCH.
15. WHATEVER DENOMINATION THAT YOU MAY CALL THE CHURCH, IS NOT GOD'S CHURCH.

BECOMING A MEMBER OF ONE OF THOSE DENOMINATIONS LISTED ABOVE, WILL NOT MAKE YOU A MEMBER OF GOD'S CHURCH.

NOTE: GOD'S CHURCH IS NOT A DENOMIATION.

....
....
....
....

Revelation 1:7.

When JESUS returns, every eye will see Him. Those who are alive at the time of JESUS CHRIST'S return, will see Him. But not everyone who sees Him will be taken to heaven. Amongst those who are alive at the time of JESUS CHRIST'S return, only 144,000 will be translated. (Revelation 7).

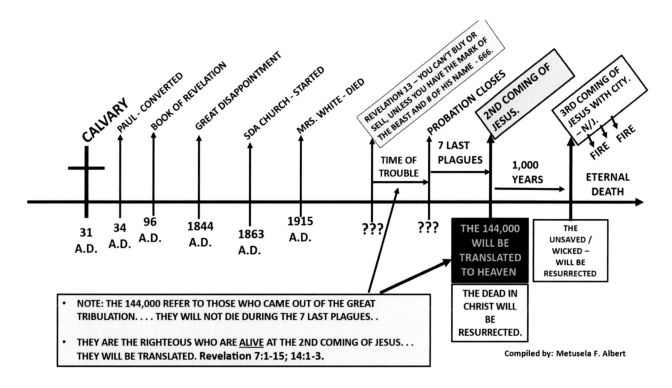

Compiled by: Metusela F. Albert

Among those who were dead during JESUS CHRIST'S return, only the righteous will be resurrected and taken to heaven. They are the great multitude.

....
....
....
....

JESUS, WHO WAS THE CREATOR OF HEAVEN AND EARTH, IS THE ONLY GOD THAT IS SITTING ON THE THRONE. HE IS COMING BACK TO TAKE HIS CHURCH TO HEAVEN WITH HIM. HE IS NOT COMING BACK TO TAKE A DENOMINATION TO HEAVEN.

....
....
....
....

GOD'S CHURCH IS <mark>NOT</mark> A DENOMINATION. THEREFORE, IF YOUR DENOMINATION CLAIMS TO BE GOD'S RENANT CHURCH, THAT IS SATANIC AND DEVILISH.

....

....

....

....

CHAPTER 11

WORSHIP IS DUE TO ELOHIM, NOT TO A TRINITY GOD.

Genesis 1:1 – In the beginning God created the heaven and the earth.

Because GOD is the Creator, therefore, worship is due to Him alone. The Hebrew word used is – ELOHIM.

Commandment # 1 in the Ten Commandments forbids the worship of other man-made gods. All man-made gods are not equal to GOD, who is self-existent.

....
....
....
....

FURTHER EXPLANATION.

Commandment # 1 in the Ten Commandments tells us to worship no other gods except the Creator. The ELOHIM who created heaven and earth is not a Trinity GOD. If our GOD is a Trinity GOD, then we are transgressing Commandment # 1.

THERE IS NO SUCH THING AS A TRINITY GOD IS SITTING ON THE THRONE, IN HEAVEN. BEWARE THAT YOU DO NOT HAVE A TRINITY GOD IN YOUR BELIEF. OTHERWISE, YOU HAVE AN IDOL GOD. AND YOU ARE ANTI-CHRIST.

....
....
....
....

CHAPTER 12

THE TRINITY GOD THEORY, IS ANTI-CHRIST.

IF you believe that <u>a TRINITY GOD</u>, is sitting on the Throne, in heaven; then <u>you are Anti-Christ.</u>

WHY?

Because, you have reduced JESUS CHRIST who was the ALPHA AND OMEGA, <u>the only GOD,</u> in heaven; to a Son of GOD that was born in heaven by the Father, with a beginning.

THE TRINITY GOD THEORY, IS DEVILISH.

WE MUST CONDEMN AND REBUKE <u>THE FALSE TRINITY GOD</u> THEORY THAT IS BEING PROMOTED BY MOST PROTESTANT CHURCHES OF THE 21ST CENTURY.

THAT IS A <u>SATANIC, ANTI-CHRIST MOVEMENT,</u> TO MAKE ERROR BECOME THE TRUTH. THAT IS AN OPEN ATTACK UPON JESUS CHRIST.

Unfortunately, most mainline Denominations (Churches) believe in a TRINITY GOD theory.

We must uplift JESUS CHRIST more aggressively against the False Trinity GOD doctrine.

The TRINITY GOD theory is transgressing Commandment # 1 where GOD says, Thou shalt have no other gods before <u>Me.</u>

....

....

....

....

CHAPTER 13

JOHN AND PAUL CONTRADICTED WHAT GOD SAID, IN GENESIS 1:1 AND ISAIAH 43:10-11.

When John wrote his gospel, he did <u>not</u> know that <u>JESUS was the ELOHIM</u> who created heaven and earth in six days and rested on the seventh day.

John 1:1 advocated the DUALITY GOD THEORY which contradicted Genesis 1:1 and Isaiah 43:10-11.

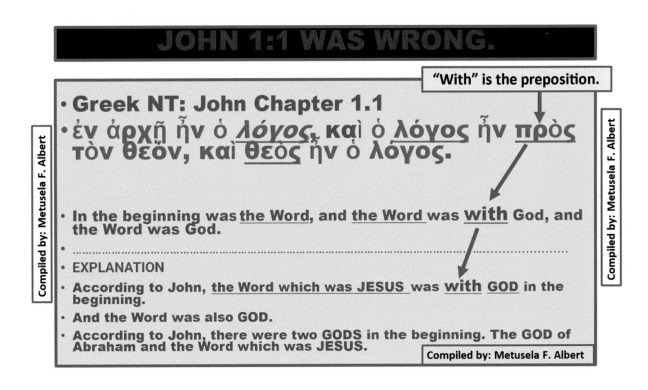

32

The disciple, John, advocated that GOD had a begotten Son in heaven – (John 3:16). What does that mean? It means that GOD the Father, and the Son (JESUS), were <u>TWO DISTINCT BEINGS</u> that existed in heaven, before the angels were created.

The Father + The Son (JESUS) = 2 DISTINCT BEINGS.

But the Old Testament speaks of <u>only One Divine Being that existed, in heaven</u>.

....
....
....
....

HOW DID PAUL CONTRADICT - GENESIS 1:1 AND ISAIAH 43:10-11?

Paul wrote in Colossians 1:15-18 that JESUS was the *first-born* of all creatures. In other words, Paul advocated the notion that JESUS had a beginning. That means, JESUS <u>cannot</u> be the Alpha and Omega, the First and the Last.

When we know the truth that JESUS was the Almighty GOD of Abraham before his INCARNATION into human flesh through Mary at Bethlehem; that helps us to notice the errors advocated by John and Paul.

....
....
....
....

<u>WHAT IS THE TRUTH ABOUT JESUS?</u>

JESUS, THE <u>ONLY GOD,</u> IS THE ONLY ONE THAT IS SITTING ON THE THRONE, IN HEAVEN.

<u>HE WAS THE ALMIGHTY GOD OF ABRAHAM WHO HUMBLY TOOK HUMAN FLESH BY THE INCARNATION PROCESS THROUGH MARY AT BETHLEHEM, AND DIED AT CALVARY AS OUR SAVIOR / SIN BEARER, TO SAVE US FROM SIN AND ETERNAL DESTRUCTION.</u>

That is the most amazing love of GOD. HE who was the Father, took human flesh through Mary at Bethlehem, and became the Son of GOD. THERE WAS <u>NO TWO DISTINCT PERSONS</u> INVOLVED IN HERE.

‹››

‹››

‹››

‹››

CHAPTER 14

JESUS, THE ONLY GOD, IS THE ONLY ONE THAT IS SITTING ON THE THRONE, IN HEAVEN.

The Scripture Reading in Revelation 4:1-11 makes it very clear. HE was the <u>ELOHIM</u> who created heaven and earth in six days and rested on the seventh day. HE was <u>the LORD of the Sabbath</u>. HE was <u>the I AM THAT I AM</u> who spoke to Moses at the Burning Bush – Exodus 3:13-14; John 5:39, 46; 8:56-58. HE was <u>the ALPH AND OMEGA, the FIRST and the LAST,</u> who spoke to disciple John, on the Island of Patmos – Revelation 21:5-7. HE was the One that died, resurrected, and lived forever. HE ascended to heaven and is coming back again.

When you come to fully understand that JESUS was the "<u>ELOHIM</u>" who created heaven and earth, you don't have to guess as to who was the One sitting on the THRONE in heaven. It is common sense. It is JESUS! There is none before and after Him. Every praise, honor, and glory must be given to Him. Amen.

....
....
....
....

So sad to say that so many Church leaders still believe in the FALSE Trinity GOD theory because they have not understood the Simple Principle of Interpreting Scripture, laid down in this Book.

Since they did <u>not</u> understand it, then don't expect the flock under their roof to understand it.

Dear Reader, You do not need to go to a Theological Seminary to learn it. In fact, the wealth of information given in this Book is greater than your four years of learning in a Seminary to understand GOD.

There are FOUR Simple Scriptures that you need to understand *before* reading Genesis 1:26. Reading the Context is so vital, yet neglected by so many Theologians and Church leaders.

WHAT ARE THE <u>FOUR SCRIPTURES</u>?

1. Genesis 1:1 – <u>GOD</u> was the CREATOR of heaven and earth in six days.
2. Genesis 1:5 – Read the <u>Singular Pronoun Word</u> mentioned to refer to the <u>Noun Word</u> – "GOD".... "HE".... <u>NOT</u> "THEY".
3. Genesis 1:10 – Read the <u>Singular Pronoun Word</u> mentioned to refer to the <u>Noun Word</u> – "GOD".... "HE".... <u>NOT</u> "THEY".
4. Genesis 1:16 – Read the <u>Singular Pronoun Word mentioned</u> to refer to the <u>Noun Word</u> – "GOD".... "HE"... <u>NOT</u> "THEY".

....
....
....
....

I repeat, when you understand the CONTEXT where the PRONOUN mentioned is – "HE," you will <u>not</u> believe again in the FALSE TRINITY GOD THEORY taken out of CONTEXT from Genesis 1:26.

Furthermore, the CONTEXT in Genesis 1:27-31 and Genesis 2:1-3, affirms the truth that <u>there is no such thing that the CREATOR of heaven and earth in six days, is a TRINITY GOD.</u>

Of course, JESUS who was the LORD of the Sabbath Day, was not, and is not, a <u>TRINITY GOD.</u>

I hope that you as the Reader, are able to understand the above explanation.

....
....
....
....

CONCLUSION

I hope this Book is helpful to your understanding and boosts your faith stronger in your belief about JESUS, our only GOD, that is sitting on the Throne, in heaven.

Thank you for purchasing and reading the Book. And thank you for sharing with your friends.

....
....
....
....

THIS IS MY 15TH BOOK.

For your information, listed below are other books I have written that may be of interest to you and your friends.

PUBLISHED ON MARCH 04, 2011

PUBLISHED ON JUNE 01, 2021

....
....
....
....

THERE IS NO TRINITY GOD IN HEAVEN.

BOOK - PUBLISHED ON DECEMBER 16, 2020.

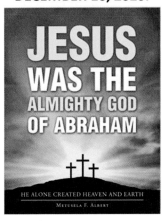

BOOK - PUBLISHED ON JANUARY 22, 2021

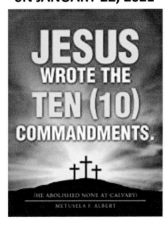

BOOK - PUBLISHED ON SEPTEMBER 12, 2021

PUBLISHED ON AUGUST 17, 2021.

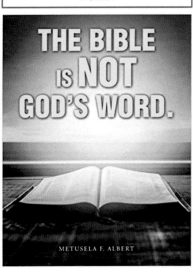

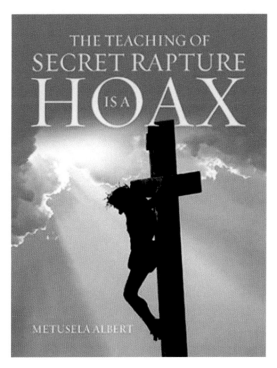

//
//
//
//

BOOK # 8

PUBLISHED ON MARCH 21, 2023.

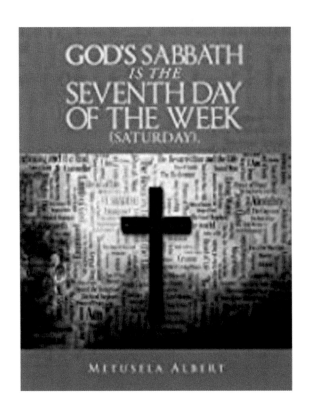

....
....
....
....

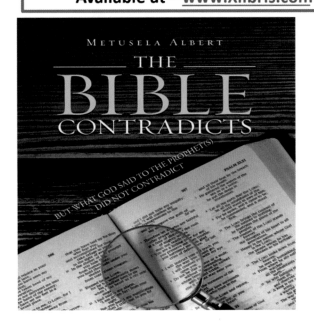

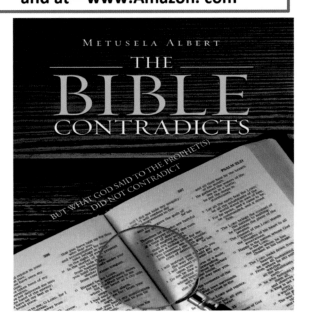

....
....
....
....

MY 10TH BOOK – THE 144,000 IN THE BOOK OF REVELATION. It is <u>a literal number</u>.

MY 11TH BOOK – SALVATION IS CONDITIONAL.

MY 12TH BOOK – GOD DID NOT HAVE A BEGOTTEN SON.

MY 13TH BOOK – WHO IS GOD'S REMNANT CHURCH?

MY 14TH BOOK – LEARN HOW TO READ AND INTERPRET SCRIPTURE.

MY 15TH BOOK – WHO IS SITTING ON THE THRONE, IN HEAVEN? This is the Book that you have in your hand.

....
....
....
....

ALL THOSE BOOKS CAN BE PURCHASED ONLINE. <u>WWW.XLIBRIS.COM and other online Book Sellers.</u>

....
....
....
....

CURRENTLY, (SEPTEMBER 30, 2024), I AM WORKING ON <u>THREE MORE BOOKS</u> AS LISTED BELOW, TO PUBLISH BEFORE DECEMBER 2024, TO FURTHER EXPOSE THE ERRORS OF THE TRINITY GOD THEORY.

Stay tuned and get hold of these Books to read the truth that your Church never told you yet since your Church is still struggling to understand How to Interpret simple Scriptures like Genesis 1:1, 1:2, and 1:26, <u>in the Context of Genesis 1:5, 10, 16. The Singular Pronouns are very clear.</u>

<u>THE THREE BOOKS I PLANNED TO WRITE AND PUBLISH BEFORE DECEMBER 31, 2024:</u>

<u>MY 16TH BOOK</u> – WHAT IS THE SPIRIT OF PROPHECY (SOP), MENTIONED IN REVELATION 19:10?

<u>MY 17TH BOOK</u> – WHO IS THE HOLY SPIRIT? <u>NOT</u> A THIRD PERSON – Genesis 1:1-3.

<u>MY 18TH BOOK</u> – THE <u>FIRST THREE TEXTS,</u> <u>MISINTERPRETED</u> BY MOST DENOMINATIONS, TO JUSTIFY THE TRINITY GOD THEORY – Genesis 1:1; 1:2, & 1:26.

....
....
....
....

Dear folks, when you know the truth, you will easily know the error(s). But if you don't know the truth, you will <u>not</u> know the error(s). It is that simple. That is why we try to learn the truth from the Book of Genesis, Chapter 1, before the New Testament. I hope you can now notice the errors easily because of the truth we have learned about JESUS, our <u>only</u> GOD, that is sitting on the THRONE, in heaven.

THERE WAS NONE BEFORE HIM, AND THERE WILL BE NONE AFTER HIM. (Isaiah 43:10-11, 15).

....
....
....
....

- THE END –

....
....
....
....

This Page is for your Notes & Information.

1. **Your Name:**
    ....
    ....

2. **The Author's Name: . . . Metusela Albert. . . . . .**

3. **The Book Title : WHO IS SITTING ON THE THRONE, IN HEAVEN?**

4. **The Date you Purchased this Book:**
    ....

5. **Which online website you purchased the Book?**
    ....

6. **What was the Price of your Book**
    ....

7. **The <u>Author's EMAIL</u> contact.** <u>Metusela_albert@yahoo.com</u>

8. **Contact the <u>Author's EMAIL</u> address, to give him – your feedback.**

9. **SHARE <u>THE BOOK TITLE(S)</u> with your friends through the social media platform – Facebook, etc.**

10. ....
    ....

11. ....
....

12. ....
....

13. ....
....

14. ....
....

15. ....
....

16. ....
....

17. ....
....

18. ....
....

19. ....
....

20. ....
....

Printed in the United States
by Baker & Taylor Publisher Services